With God, All Things Are Possible!

Copyright 2017
All rights reserved

ISBN 978-0-9985225-9-3
ISBN
All rights reserved. No part of this publication may be reproduced in any means, in any way, without the permission, in writing, from the copyright owner.
A product of SkookumBooks.com 864 236 8058

Dedication: To all my students, at Madison Elementary, Sandusky, Ohio, who saw how much I loved history. Every once-in-a- while, someone would remark, "You really like this stuff"! We had some very interesting times, talking, and discovering, and learning about our history!

Acknowledgment: None of the books, we have published, would exist, if our son, Stephen, hadn't done all the work needed to self-publish. The topics I have written about, doesn't seem to interest publishers. I have lived long enough to see there is a need to have a conversation with our young people, about subjects which will make them or break them. Talking can bring an awareness, and perhaps alert them that there are many choices to make as they grow in wisdom! I believe our country's future, and our democracy is going to be sorely tested. Our children will determine the outcome. There are some very foolish people about, who don't realize the damage they are doing to our country. Because they have access to a microphone, they are making statements which show their brains and mouths are out of sink!

Skookum Books Charms

The beautiful butterfly, that graces our flowers and bushes, goes through a mysterious, and magical change in becoming an adult! The Greeks believed each time a butterfly emerges from its cocoon, a new human soul is born. Legend has it that whispering a wish to a butterfly, then releasing it to carry the wish to heaven, will make the wish come true! Perhaps this is when they acquire little clouds on their wings. The butterfly is a symbol of fresh life, happiness, and joy! The "night" butterfly, the moth, is attracted to a flame and light, just like our souls are attracted to heavenly truths!

Hummingbirds are active, beautiful additions to our gardens, who give us a sense of life, nature's beauty, and fresh life! These "flying jewels", flit from flower to flower, picking up and delivering pollen, so that life can continue. Hummingbirds open the heart and show the truth of beauty! It brings laughter and enjoyment and the magic of being alive! The hummingbird stands for spreading love and joy!

History,

Love It and Learn

or

Hate It and Harm

Betty Lou Rogers

History is a real, true story
No one can change it, no matter how hard they try,
What happened, really happened, good or bad,
Might as well face it, be happy, or mad, or sad!

History tells it, like it is,
It's actual and factual and true,
If some will change a part, it becomes a tale,
It's not history then, just a story, for sale!

People can blame, alibi, excuse, and deny,
Smart people will take heed and learn,
History can teach valuable lessons,
Like, what works or not, what must be earned!

Our story that tells what happened in the past,
Should be treasured for the information it gives,
People suffered and died, they endured misery and pain,
They made many decisions, not for self-gain!

It's easy to blame, second guess, find fault,
With our ancestors, for how they lived,
Without research or study we can't possibly know,
The circumstances they met, or what they had to forego!

Heroes emerged, from acts of courage and daring,
They were struggling for the good they could do,
These people were honored for valor and heart,
Many gave up their lives, being the worst part!

Now, to pull down memorials, in memory of brave men,
Is irreverent toward the deeds which were done,
Remembering these lives, is a sacred duty, no less,
We should express, our gratitude, for they made us so blessed!

People don't appreciate democracy,
It's government by the people, and for them,
It's the fairest and most honest way to lead,
It's freedom and opportunity, it's great indeed!

Let's look back, to see how our country began,
Something this good, didn't happen by chance,
Strong, courageous people came to this sod,
They wanted freedom, safety, and trusted in God!

At a time in history, the world was so dark,
People were in danger, were starving, living in filth,
God must have thought these people needed to know,
About a place across the ocean, a new place to go!

So God, must have carved out America,
A place of beauty, nature's bounty, and peace,
A place to go, a place to make a safe home,
A place to honor, and stay, never to roam!

During this time, America was unknown,
No one even knew it was there,
It lay across a wide, treacherous ocean,
And these unhappy people, didn't have a notion!

A man called Christopher Columbus,
Was daring and a man unafraid,
He wanted to show all the people,
Our world was round, as it was made!

He told all the people, who would listen,
He would sail toward the west,
And if he kept on going,
He'd be back home, at best!

By doing that, he discovered this New World,
People became interested in this foreign place,
Their living was bad, this offered a better life,
This different place would free them from strife!

It took rugged people to venture forth,
For they knew not, what lay ahead,
But they were ready to go, even felt some glee,
To this New World adventure, they would flee!

This new land, was a good answer,
For those who wanted to change their lives,
They'd have to work hard, take care of themselves,
They were taking a chance, to grow and survive!

These daring people, wanted to live free,
They wanted to be able to speak their minds,
They wanted to worship God, as they chose,
They wanted a safe place to raise their kind!

They first had to build themselves a home,
They had to provide all the food for their needs,
But the biggest job, they had on their hands,
Was to build up a nation, a place that was grand!

When our country was young, a mere babe,
Brave men wondered how to proceed,
Intelligent men who were smart and aware,
Knew the rules of our country should be honest and fair!

These people who settled our land from the start,
Had no idea of all the needs they must meet,
They were probably unsure, but doing their best,
Willing to serve, perhaps, truly distressed!

Do you know you live in a wonderful land?
Are you thankful for those people who made it so?
It took a lot of blood, sweat, and tears to help it grow,
Men died, families suffered, more than we'll ever know!

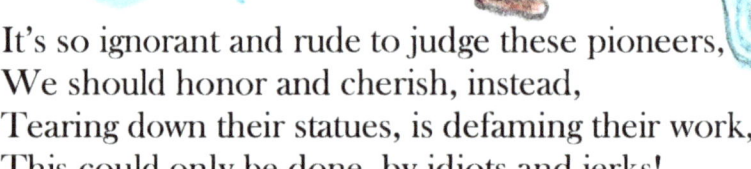

It's so ignorant and rude to judge these pioneers,
We should honor and cherish, instead,
Tearing down their statues, is defaming their work,
This could only be done, by idiots and jerks!

It's better to understand, than be ignorant and rude,
It's smarter to study them, and learn what they thought,
We could find out how, and what, even why they did,
But covering over, tearing down, and burning won't fit!

These early people, were paving the way,
For us to follow, and improve what they began,
But to not appreciate their hard work, and their tears,
Is a disgrace, a shame, and a stain on those years!

Our country is great, it's one of a kind,
Thanks to our ancestors who made it this way,
Nowhere on earth is there life so divine,
The patriots of the past, made our country so fine!

We should honor and revere these heroes of old,
They worried, and sacrificed, they bled, some died,
Our country is the result of their work and their wear.
Their struggling, many times, were on a wing and a prayer!

If you can't appreciate the patriots of the past,
You aren't material to be a patriot today,
For they did many things as they worried and talked,
And they did what was needed, they walked the walk!

This land was a haven, a safe place to live,
But it had many, many problems to solve,
It was a wish, a dream for the tired and poor,
For the huddled masses, yearning to be free!

Good leaders were needed, good decisions too,
Someone had to step up and be strong,
They had to protect liberty, and keep people safe,
They had to find the right answers, never to stray!

These new Americans were not trained at all,
In how to launch a nation with freedom and heart,
They didn't want a king to run our land,
They wanted unselfish leaders, who were wise and smart!

We all should treasure our country, our home,
We've made mistakes, but we mostly succeed,
Our patriots have worked to make this land like no other,
We have freedom and privilege and love for our brothers!

These early Americans who lived long ago,
Served our country loyally, by guiding its way,
They had to deal with the problems they faced,
Nation building is hard, and must be sustained!!

It's unfair to judge what these people did,
We don't know what difficulties they had,
Perhaps they were the ones to do, what had to be done,
Perhaps, they, like no others, developed the right outcome!

A patriot will sacrifice anything for good,
A patriot is true to his deeds and his words,
A patriot places his countries welfare, first,
For his country, a patriot will suffer the worst!

Tearing down monuments from the past doesn't work,
For there was a good reason to place them there,
Monuments don't honor thieves, rascals, or spies,
Better find out all the goodness that was done, and why!

Desecrating our flag, pulling down memories of the past,
Is so stupid, but simpletons, will try,
They wouldn't know of the bravery shown,
They wouldn't recognize courage, even full-blown!

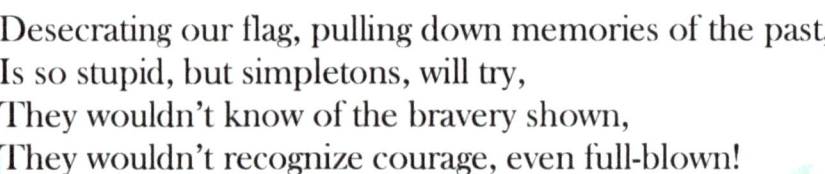

Let's face it, let's grow up, let's win,
Why not be proud of our country as it improves,
We've found some things wrong, mistakes, and miscues,
But changing, correcting, improving renews!

We can be proud of our country, tis true,
We have everything, more than any place we can name!
And our freedom is special, people are valued and blest,
We'd rather play games, have some fun, than protest!!

We are the nation of compassion,
Everyone comes our way for help,
May we always be generous and kind,
And keep our merciful ways, in mind!

Despots and dictators, tyrants, and kings,
Would first destroy all evidence of the past,
But those who destroy, what once was so cool,
Are dishonoring, insulting the importance of rules

History recalls brave souls of the past,
For their courage, and unyielding ways,
They didn't give up, they were persistent and just,
They achieved what they could, and did what they must!

Back in time, cowboys rode the range,
Herding and protecting the cattle, was their job,
They could get lost, stolen, or wander away,
And this could happen, most everyday!

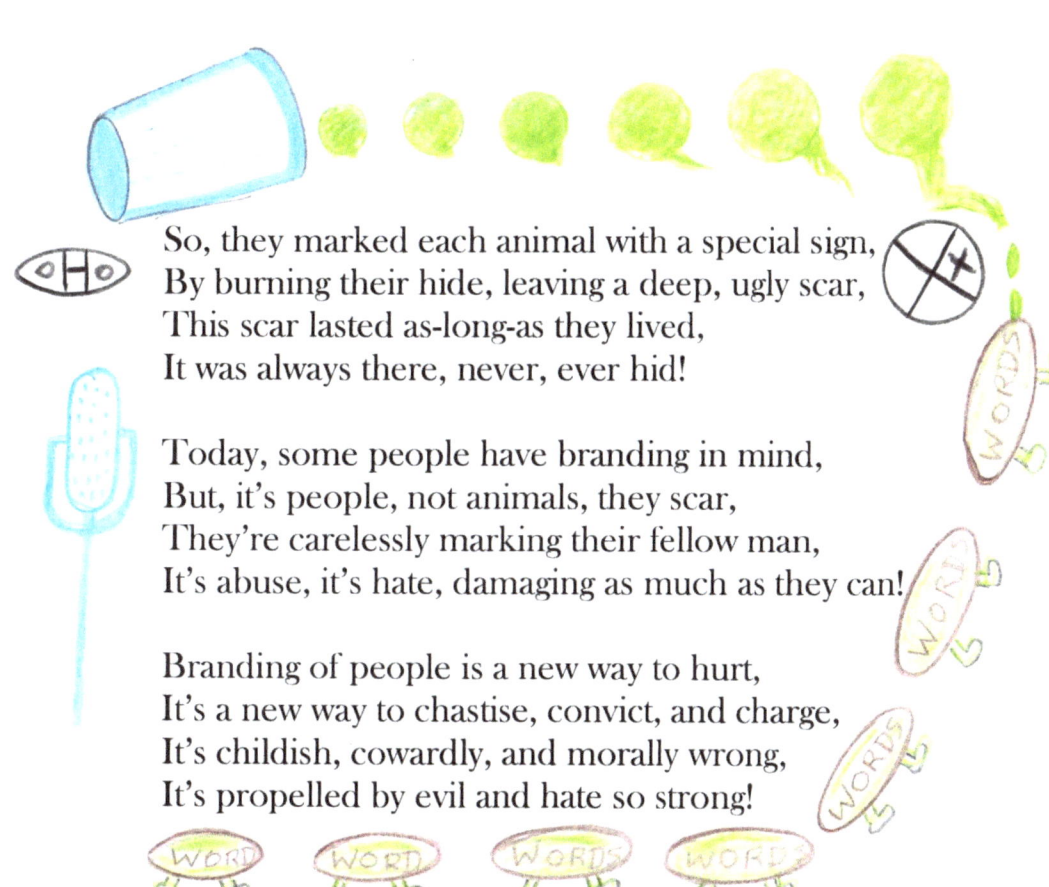

So, they marked each animal with a special sign,
By burning their hide, leaving a deep, ugly scar,
This scar lasted as-long-as they lived,
It was always there, never, ever hid!

Today, some people have branding in mind,
But, it's people, not animals, they scar,
They're carelessly marking their fellow man,
It's abuse, it's hate, damaging as much as they can!

Branding of people is a new way to hurt,
It's a new way to chastise, convict, and charge,
It's childish, cowardly, and morally wrong,
It's propelled by evil and hate so strong!

Our flag has been raised, many a time,
By courageous and brave, bloodied men,
At Fort McHenry, would you have helped,
To protect Old Glory, during the violence?

Would you have helped at the Siegfried Line?
One man out of ten was killed or hurt,
But our flag showed brave Americans were there
Fighting for our democratic rule and welfare!

On a tiny island, only five miles long,
Iwo Jima offered airstrips, for our planes,
The fighting was terrific, lasted a month,
Would you have helped raise our flag, that way?

Okinawa

Iwo Jima

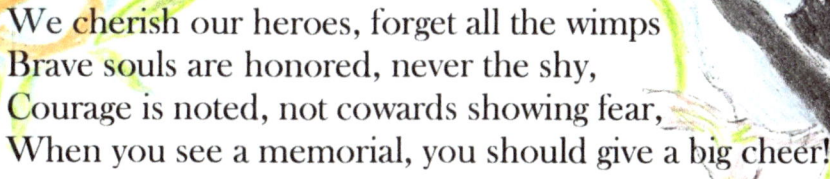

We cherish our heroes, forget all the wimps
Brave souls are honored, never the shy,
Courage is noted, not cowards showing fear,
When you see a memorial, you should give a big cheer!

Many people have limited perceptions,
Of all the things they can achieve,
Our country offers unlimited chances,
To succeed and fulfill, carry out, and enhance!

So, believe in what's possible, with effort and grit,
Believe in yourself, have faith that you're "it",
You can achieve what you want, if you want it enough,
Might take some hard work, hang in there, be tough!

Perhaps when God created the earth,
He wanted to show a bit of heaven to all,
He gave us a land of plenty and peace,
And we're living under His trust, to say the least!

Growing up is the name of the game,
It's showing your thinking and actions are sure,
Understanding our past, believing in what's ahead,
Willing to solve problems, finding answers that's best!

Growing up is sharing and caring with strangers and friends,
Showing love and compassion for all,
No jealous thoughts or hateful acts, only thankful conditions,
Proud of our country, having no evil remissions!

Down through the ages, we've had to defend,
Our country, its values, and goals,
Our flag, as it waves, stands for honor and worth,
Are you ready to guard and protect this land of your birth?

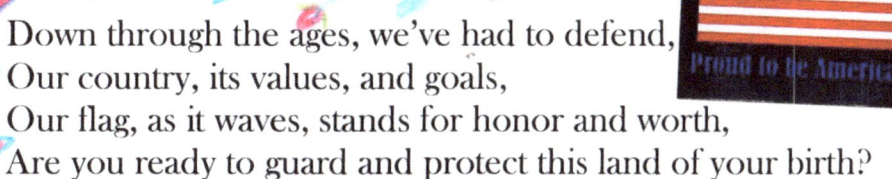

What are you doing to be a good American?
Are you looking for something to get, or to give?
Our country gives you the right to be and do,
It gives you the dignity, equality, and freedom to be you!

You have the freedom to choose what you want,
You also are free to choose what you do, how to act,
This sets you apart, and recognizes your worth,
You know good from bad, you choose, based on fact!

A man once said, "It's surprising what can be done,
When you don't know it's not possible to do",
You do the undoable, you invent, you create,
You achieve the impossible, educate, and relate!

Always remember - - - Never forget,

America is your homeland,
"Twas won with blood and strife,
So, cherish all your freedoms,
And guard them with your life!

The American's Creed

I believe in the United States of America as a government of the people, by the people, for the people; whose just powers are derived from the consent of the governed; a democracy in a republic; a sovereign Nation of many sovereign States ; a perfect Union, one and inseparable; established upon the principles of freedom, equality, justice, and humanity for which American patriots sacrificed their lives and fortunes.

I therefore believe it is my duty to my country to love it, to support its Constitution; to obey its laws; to respect its flag and to defend it against all enemies.

William Tyler Page

About the Author

Betty Lou Rogers is a retired fourth grade teacher from Madison Elementary School in Sandusky, Ohio. Her strategy for success was simple. Engage! Work together! Be active learners! Then employ her "one more chance" philosophy!

Betty Lou Rogers grew up in rural northwestern Ohio, graduating from Fremont Ross High School. She married her childhood sweetheart and raised three sons. During this time, she returned to college where she graduated with a B. S. Degree in Elementary Education from Bowling Green State University, in Bowling Green, Ohio. She was a member of the prestigious educational society, Kappa Delta Pi.

While teaching at Madison School, Mrs. Rogers was keenly aware of what children needed, both as a group and as individuals, in effectual learning in the classroom. She also had the intuition to know how to accomplish this by challenging her students to be active learners, as opposed to the sit, listen, and absorb approach! Always have lesson material in front of the student, so they are actively participating in the lesson, never pushing the child beyond their ability, but always working toward the best they can do! Often times the student is awakened to and surprised by their own ability. Mrs. Rogers' most telling educational approach was offering the children "one more chance" to learn and succeed, by giving open-book tests!

Tests show what the student hasn't learned! "My job is to give the children every opportunity to learn." This strategy caused her students to become more familiar with the contents and location of information in their books. This offering, enabled them to find the answer, complete the test, and learn what was missed before. These answers could even be more meaningful to them! When parents found this out, there was no excuse for a failing grade!

Mrs. Rogers was also a Jennings Scholar, which honored and rewarded teachers in the elementary classroom. The Jennings Foundation provides a means for greater accomplishment, on the part of teachers, with the hope it would result in greater recognition for those in the teaching profession within the public school system.

Mrs. Rogers and her husband chose to retire in beautiful South Carolina. They are members of Advent United Methodist Church in Simpsonville, S.C. Besides writing, she loves her sewing and crafts, and gardening! Mrs. Rogers and her husband have four granddaughters, and seven great-grandchildren! After twenty-seven years of teaching, Mrs. Rogers philosophy for success has permeated the American landscape through her students in both academic and professional fields. Her love for teaching and writing, can never be equaled in any way, except her hope for students to find her writing truly illuminating!

New publications coming:

The Parables, Jesus's Timely Tales!

Kate Earns Her MBA in Manners, Behavior, Attitude!

Chris Earns His MBA in Manners, Behavior, Attitude!

Acquiring The Human Skills of Thinking, Saying, and Doing, for Teens!

A Medley of Options for the "Not Yet Old" Set!

God and Country. Two Sets of Laws For Teens!

The Human Dilemma of the Young, The Scramble for Power, Approval, and Money, (Ecclesiastes)

Teens, Consider the Circumstances and Consequences!

Law and Order for Teens: Ignore or Restore!

ABC's For Teens, and What They Mean!

Loves Flowers, Hates Weeds!

So, You Think We Shouldn't Have Dropped "The Bomb"?

For fun: Bossy Susie Saucy   and Capricious Caleb O'Connor